FINDING A BETTER WAY

BY

DANA DIAZ BERMUDEZ

Hasmark Publishing
www.hasmarkpublishing.com

Disclaimer

This book is designed to provide information and motivation to our readers. It is sold with the understanding that the publisher is not engaged to render any type of psychological, legal, or any other kind of professional advice. The content of each article is the sole expression and opinion of its author, and not necessarily that of the publisher. No warranties or guarantees are expressed or implied by the publisher's choice to include any of the content in this volume. Neither the publisher nor the individual author(s) shall be liable for any physical, psychological, emotional, financial, or commercial damages, including, but not limited to, special, incidental, consequential or other damages. Our views and rights are the same: You are responsible for your own choices, actions, and results.

Permission should be addressed in writing to Dana Diaz Bermudez at danadiazbermudez@outlook.com

Editor: Harshita Sharma harshita@hasmarkpublishing.com

Creative Director: Anne Karklins anne@hasmarkpublishing.com
Book Design: Amit Dey amit@hasmarkpublishing.com

ISBN 13: 978-1-77482-120-6
ISBN 10: 1774821206

If you're standing at the edge right now, I beg you
to step back and read this book. I wrote it to show
you that you deserve another chance to try
something else.

This is a book to activate your inspiration to never
give up on yourself. There is always something better
out there for you if you are willing
and able to try.

DEDICATION

Thank you so much to my amazing husband Danys and our beautiful children Daniel, Danfranco, and Danaleez. You guys were my inspiration to keep going when I never thought I would break through my paradigms. Thank you so much for encouraging me to keep going. Your belief made me believe in myself and helped me achieve my goals. Thank you to all my mentors and coaches who stayed with me on this journey because they saw something in me that I could not. Thank you for lending me your trust and readily offering your help every time I asked. I am so grateful for all the wonderful people I have attracted into my life over the past eighteen months.

My life has been completely changed forever.

FOREWORD

Finding a Better Way was written by the author because she did precisely that; she found a better way to live her life and now she can help you live a better life too.

Everyone has a story, but not everyone will choose to learn from their own experience and not everyone makes a conscious decision to positively change their life for the better. Creating a positive change doesn't mean that there is something "wrong" with you or that you are incomplete. It is a natural desire to have a better life. This feeling for more or better is inherent within all human beings. Dana simply decided to do something about making her life better because she was dissatisfied. I learned many years ago that dissatisfaction can stimulate growth.

More than forty years ago, I decided to find a better way as well. At the time, I was a young woman, and my life was a mess. I didn't understand success at the time. Fortunately, I found an extraordinary mentor/teacher and followed his advice. Please know this, as this is VERY important: It isn't enough to study the materials, by watching the videos, reading the books, or attending the events. You MUST incorporate success strategies into your daily practice, or you won't get the results you are looking for.

As a prosperity mentor I choose to distill success principles into the most simplistic approach— because the truth is, when you feel good, you attract good. Also, the principles for success will work for anyone who has the desire. It also doesn't matter where you came from, or what has happened or not happened in the past. Your success is absolutely guaranteed, but you must do the work.

As you are reading Dana's book, she'll take you on her own journey of challenges, and share with you how she overcame them. Most people would love success to be a straight line, like going from point A to point B. But the truth is, success isn't like that. It is more like a roller coaster … you'll have ups, and you'll have downs, and you must learn how to enjoy the entire ride.

If you are either reading this book online or holding it in your hands, you have an opportunity right now to change your life for the better. From personal experience, and from helping millions of people live their dream life, your successful future is waiting for you. Make an irrevocable decision today that you are committed to your success. Invest the time to think about how you would love to be living your life. Think of goals that inspire you and stretch you. Write down your goals in the present tense, as if you've already achieved them. Name it and claim it, as my good friend would suggest. The best thing you can do today is to make a commitment that you are going to dedicate your life to success. The rewards are truly worth it.

—Peggy McColl,
New York Times Best-selling Author

CONTENTS

PREFACE

I was inspired to write this book because I have always made it out to the other side. I have always found the light at the end of the tunnel so to speak. I want to empower others to do the same. Never give up on yourself, whatever you're going through—mental health issues, a breakup, a loss of someone, addiction, divorce, abuse, assault, business failure, losing all your money, losing all your friends, feeling like you have no one. Anything you have gone through or are currently going through, the principles in this book can help you make it to the other side. These are the steps I followed every time, consciously and unconsciously, to find the light for myself. I have been through many things. In the first chapter, I map out the negative things that led me into my depression with anxiety that landed me on medication. And in the following chapters, I lay out my success map for you to change your life as I have changed mine. We all have differing results, but if I can do it, YOU CAN DO IT.

CHAPTER 1

ABOUT ME AND THE REASONS BEHIND WRITING THIS BOOK

Some people are born leaders. They grew up with parents who made over $100,000 each in a year. They grew up in nice houses, wearing nice clothing, eating rich foods, with boats and vacations. When they graduate college with a degree or a master's, they move forward to work hard and earn good money. The only thing they think is wrong with them is self-image. They marry a great spouse right out of the gate and their happily ever after starts.

Then there are other people who were born to mediocre parents who never even finished school, never mind having a master's degree. They have parents who work very hard but never had the type of jobs that would earn them over $100,000 combined. Their parents gave up all the toys, trailers, boats, Ski-Doos, and cars, just to own a house. Then, finally, after years of struggling, they can afford a vacation per year.

Both scenarios involve hard-working, law-abiding citizens. Both have houses, cars, kids, and lots of stuff. But the big difference is that one household works from nine in the morning until five at night, and the other works from five in the morning until nine at night.

That is what I grew up believing. Above average people worked a lot more hours than the average person. That's why I didn't want to be rich because I wanted my life to be my life. I didn't want to work my life away.

Before I got married, I lived to work. I was in a lot of debt, and I was chasing the almighty dollar. I had to have a job. My parents told me so. The guys I dated told me so. My friends and family all had jobs. It was normal. After my first child, I started working to live, and that's when my story completely changed.

I grew up seeing prosperity all around me. I loved cars, and it was odd back then for a female to be into street racing. Now, the racing industry is saturated with women, but back then, it wasn't very common. I felt unique. I was surrounded by men with what I thought was a lot of money. They drove very nice, expensive cars and talked about money a lot while hanging out at a parking lot at night. Some of them would bring their wives and others left their wives at home and brought their girlfriends. I saw abundance all around me. These guys weren't struggling at all. They talked about their big homes and they always wore nice brand name clothing. Their wives were so pretty. I never understood why any of them would cheat on a woman like the one they had. Even after she'd had two of the guy's kids, she was still insanely attractive. The wives had nice handbags and big, beautiful diamond rings, and their hair and makeup were perfect.

Yet, there I was. Young, skinny, and naturally beautiful. I never wore makeup, and I still don't. I just never felt like I needed it. I knew I wasn't like them. I was driving my mom's old beat-up Ford Tempo. And they were driving Mustangs, Corvettes, and Vipers. They had race cars and they had their other cars that they would drive to work and back. It was incredible to see. Maybe that's why I loved being around them. It was a totally different life than the one I had at home.

I believe that's what changed my life when I thought about money. My parents were not well off, but they always had everything they needed, and I never went without. They went on vacations a couple of times a year. The fridge was always full. But when it came to me, it felt like everything was hard. I dropped out of high school. I was bullied, made fun of, beat up, sexually harassed. I wasn't focused. I had anxiety. By the time I turned seventeen, I was a high school dropout and on anti-anxiety medication, and I didn't fit in very well. The friends I made were never the cool kids.

I have struggled with mental health issues for as long as I can remember. When I was a kid, my teachers thought it would be better for my growth and development if I was put in a special ed class because I was too hyper as well as a classroom distraction. When being in a small portable with three other boys didn't work, they tried putting me in a small room in the front office, where it was just big enough to fit a desk and a small chair with one adult standing in front of the desk. When all of their efforts still didn't make me conform to the way they wanted me to act, then I was put on medication at a young age to calm me down. Keep in mind that all these events happened to me before I was eight years old.

I was preprogrammed by most of the adults in my life to believe that I wasn't good enough. I was unworthy of being in a normal classroom. I was unworthy of living my life the way I saw fit. Happy and hyper was my style, and to be honest, it still is in my late thirties. My mom realized that the medication was not a good fit for me because I wasn't eating properly and I wasn't feeling like myself AT ALL. She began refusing to give me the pills months later. My mother put me in anything I enjoyed just to get my energy out. I was in gymnastics, swimming, Air Cadets, and I really enjoyed playing all sports at school, which landed me the nickname of Tomboy. When I was ten, we moved from a big city to a small town where everyone knew each other. I wasn't accepted by the kids in the new school. I was made fun of daily and bullied often. I would make friends that would use me for entertainment and make fun of me behind my back. They would sleep over at my house on the weekend and by Monday morning, I was the joke of the school. After two years of this, my mom did what any good mother would do and switched me from the Catholic school to the public school. I would have been about twelve years old at that time. While all of this was happening to me at school, my parents, who had their own issues, were raising me on the other end. They did the very best they could with what they were brought up with.

My dad was an only child just like me and he had a very physically, emotionally, and mentally abusive upbringing himself. He came to Canada when he was nine years old. He was raised by a mother who was filled with love and a father who was filled with pain and suffering from his own past. Unfortunately, my dad wasn't treated very well by his father, and by the age of twelve, he was protecting his mother from domestic abuse. I will say that my grandfather was very good to me, and I have many wonderful memories of him before he passed away at the old age of ninety. My grandfather lived a great life, the life that he wanted. He was fun and loved to drink, and from what I heard, he was always the life of the party. My dad wasn't as lucky as I was. He never met anyone to help him overcome his past and he still suffers from a victim mentality to this day. My father has done many years of therapy, but they don't treat him. They just bring up all the pain and suffering for my dad all over again. My mother, on the other hand, was physically, emotionally, and mentally abused by her three siblings. She was born and raised by, in my opinion, wonderful people who both had huge families. At that time, my mom, her siblings, and all their cousins were raising themselves while the adults got together regularly to play cards, smoke, drink, and be merry. The kids went off without any supervision. Again, my mother did the very best she could with the knowledge she had as well. She always showed me that she loved me but as I got older, it started feeling like conditional love. Both of my parents had their own beliefs and habits. Not all of their habits were bad; both of my parents have always been very hard-working and law-abiding citizens. I never went without. If anything, people would call me spoiled because I was the only child and my parents loved to travel and brought me with them until I turned fourteen. My parents always had two reliable cars and would replace them when they needed to. We lived in a nice area where I went to school. They were middle-class people, but they had everything they needed. Not necessarily everything they wanted, but they did indeed have everything they needed. They both held jobs that they hated for a very long time. My mom loved her work, but her coworkers were mean. For twenty years, my mom worked for the same company, and for ten of those years, her supervisor emotionally abused her, gave her his work and took credit for it, and didn't pay her what she was worth. After years of her supervisor threatening her weekly that she was going to get let go from her job if she didn't do the extra work without pay, it finally started to show up in her poor health. When she got sick and had to leave work to have major surgery, they fired her. They told her that after twenty years of service, her position was dissolved. My mother had never been away from her job for more than a couple of weeks. My dad still works for the same company that he has worked with for over thirty-nine years, which makes him sick in all areas of his life. His mental health suffers along with his physical body. He is an alcoholic and knows it but says that he can't stop. He is very negative and miserable. He would never quit that job because he believes no one will hire him and he only has a couple more years to work until he can retire. With these little details about my parents and their upbringing, I am attempting to give you a small picture of my environment growing up. I was raised by hurt people. They tried not to, but I was emotionally and mentally abused until I became aware of it after thirty-six years. To me, it was normal.

I am telling you this so you can see that I wasn't raised in a great environment by any means. And I want you to know that however you were raised, whatever you have gone through, you still have a chance to change and make your own life beautiful. This universe truly wants all of us to have the best of what life has to offer. We must believe that we can achieve it. And always know that we have the universe on our side.

I am telling you the absolute truth when I say I STRUGGLED with this material. I believed in it wholeheartedly because, over the years, I have read about it and watched movies about it—the thoughts become things revelation. I just didn't know how to apply it to my own life. I watched many others create amazing lives for themselves while I stayed in the same spot, with the same patterns, along with my negative attitude. I produced really good results for a couple of months. I purchased a program and I started studying it daily. I bought my dream SUV. I bought the most expensive purse I had ever owned. I got new clothes and a new hairdo to make me feel like the person I wanted to become. Then, I slipped back into my old patterns just like my study booklet said I would because I didn't change any of my beliefs, and because I went out and spent all that money. When I fell back into my old habits, I hated the way it felt. I felt like I screwed up my family's future. I felt like a loser and an absolute failure. Those strong feelings put me into a deep depression for months. Clawing my way back out of this mess I called my life, I kept getting back up. I kept making new decisions. I kept trying, all because I hated my life. And for that very short time that I did improve, I felt so good about myself and my life and everything around me. I felt like I could be, do, or have anything I wanted. It was so empowering. I wanted that feeling back, PRONTO!!

I did not enjoy getting out of bed in the morning. It took me eight months just to figure out what my deep-rooted beliefs were and why I kept getting the same results. Every time I moved forward, it would last a couple of weeks, and then I would fall back to my old ways again. I kept asking the same questions to many different people and I kept getting the same answers. It was all in my thinking and my beliefs.

Essentially what I heard was that it was all "in my head." It was all my fault. I was a failure. I couldn't even get a handle over my thoughts to create a different day. Since I can remember, my mother has been reminding me of how I had to take every swimming class twice because I wanted to be perfect, and my dad has been telling me that I always had to learn things the hard way. Because of this, I believed I was a failure. That's why my results were not changing, because my core belief was that I couldn't do anything right. Even though I had many things in my life to prove I wasn't, I still felt like a loser. In any case, every part of my life showed that I believed I was unworthy. I lost job after job. I went through many boyfriends. I didn't have a great life at home because my dad was so strict about everything. I guess because he couldn't control his own life, he felt gratification controlling mine. I was allowed two pairs of shoes downstairs in the hall closet and two coats, because he would complain that I was taking over the house. I was bound to my 10×10 bedroom because my father never made me feel welcome in my own home. I wasn't allowed to buy anything expensive because I was paying off my education loan while I worked two jobs for four years. There is so much more that I could write about to show you the amount of mental and emotional abuse I grew up with and accepted as normal because I didn't know any better.

This is about how I went from a world filled with anxiety to really enjoying everything about my life. I hope you choose this path for yourself as well.

In 2013, I married a wonderful man with many of his own beliefs and patterns. He is Cuban-born and raised, and grew up very poor. My husband was born in 1988, and when the dissolution of the Soviet Union happened in December of 1991, it devastated Cuba because they stopped trading. My husband's family had money but there was nothing to buy. The country stayed like that until he was about twelve. I'm sure you can see where my husband's thinking comes from. My husband and I met in Cuba while my parents and I were on vacation.

That was five months after I had broken up with a man that I had been living with for about a year and a half, but unstably dating for about four years. We were both emotionally unavailable to each other. He loved a woman that he grew up with, but she didn't love him back, and I was still in love with my ex-boyfriend, who was my first real adult relationship. That guy mentally messed me up big time. He didn't physically abuse me, but he abused me emotionally and mentally. When he finally dumped me for the last time two weeks before Christmas, I was nothing of a person. That's why I attracted the unavailable man. I seem to attract men that best resemble how I feel when I meet them. My husband was no different. I had spent five months on my own, building myself back up to a place where I could look at myself in the mirror with dignity. I was figuring out who I was, and I started loving myself. When I met my husband on that beautiful sunny Tuesday morning, we were both very charming towards each other. We were both very beautiful people, fit and taking care of ourselves. On the outside, we were perfect human beings. But on the inside, we both felt we weren't good enough. That week was wonderful. We had both checked all the boxes that we were looking for in a serious companion. I spent four days with him, and I just knew I wanted to be with him. I had no idea how it was going to work, but I wanted to bring him home with me. I guess he felt the same way because he emailed me ten days after I came back home.

We dated for three months. Then he proposed to me on my second trip. I happily said yes. Six months after that we were married. I sponsored him to come to Canada so we could start our life together. I made a deal with him. If he didn't like it in Canada after two years, I would move to Cuba with him. I had lived with him and his family for three months before he came to Canada, so I knew what I was getting into. Upon his arrival to Canada in October 2013, it was our worst winter on record in twenty-two years. Needless to say, he did not adjust very well at all. Our lives moved very quickly, and he suffered every time something changed. Even when it was his own doing, it still affected him badly. He missed his family back in Cuba deeply. He went through culture shock on several occasions. He would play video games for hours, then sleep and go to work. He would rearrange his wallet several times in a month, and it would always look the same. He would take out all of his clothes from the dresser drawers, fold everything, and put it back in the same place he took it out from. It was hard for me to watch and not be able to help him through it. It was the worst feeling of helplessness. He felt guilt daily for the first couple of years. He believed we should be there with his family helping them because they were getting older. Every year, around the same time in the winter months, he would get culture shock and feel homesick and attempt to force me to move there with him. He even tried to leave us several times but never made it past the airport. I had a strong belief that my children needed to be educated in Canada so they would have a bright future. After we had kids, we made a new deal. We would wait until the children turned eighteen, after they finished high school, and then we would move to Cuba for the winter months. Let's go back a bit so you can get a general understanding of my marriage and my belief systems that seemed to be an emotional roller coaster.

When I arrived in Canada with my new husband, we lived with my parents for three weeks. We got the most perfect little one-bedroom apartment. It was ground level, so I had my sunshine. It was spacious, and we spent a lot of time and effort cleaning and painting it so it would be livable. Then, to our surprise, two weeks later I found out I was pregnant with our oldest son. Neither one of us were ready. I hadn't even found a job yet. We didn't even get a honeymoon stage because of our immigration situation. Before pregnancy, I was very sensitive to smells, so much so that it caused me to have issues with jobs and coworkers. When I got pregnant, I couldn't stand any smells. The people who lived upstairs smoked marijuana in the house and cooked fish at least three times a week. It was awful. We lived there for three months and had to move. My husband had just learned how to take the bus. We found a nice three-bedroom house that was within biking distance to my husband's work and closer to my parents. It was a nice place, but he hated how much we were paying for rent. While I was pregnant, we fought all the time about everything. We went back to see his parents just before I was no longer allowed to fly, and his dad sat him down and had the man talk. Whatever he said worked, because my husband came home a changed man. He was in a better mood. He tried harder to accept the culture. He even made a few friends. He talked to me more about what he was experiencing with the changes in our lives. My husband was born to be a father. I, on the other hand, was worried about how I would do being a mother. It was never something I dreamed of or thought of until I met my husband. He wanted children (two boys to be exact). I was in labor for 103 hours and then I was finally admitted to the hospital and given an emergency C-section because our son was already a week late, and he wasn't coming. It turned out that he was face up, so he wasn't in the right spot for birth. We stayed with my parents for four weeks after he was born. I had problems breastfeeding, which made me feel like a failure as a woman. The adjustments of being a family were hard on both of us. He was feeling guilty because his family couldn't enjoy their grandson and I was experiencing postpartum depression and had no idea how to deal with it. I was so emotional. I would cry over everything, and I never slept. My husband worked nights and my son had colic. I was awake until 4 a.m. most nights and then when my husband got home, I would want to spend time with him, and when he was sleeping, I would play with the baby and clean the house and do laundry. Right after my son was born, we started looking for a house to buy with my parents so they could grow old, and we would have help. We found the most perfect raised bungalow for all of us to live in and bought it together. My parents moved in October 2014 and then we renovated the basement to add a bathroom and a kitchen so we could live there, and we moved in January 2015 when our lease was over. I can't tell you how many things went wrong with all of it—the renovation, the living situation—it just didn't work. They helped with my son but when my son was ten months old, I found out I was pregnant again. The pregnancy didn't work for my parents. They were very unhappy, and I was very defensive. On top of all the drama at home, I returned to work when my son was a year old. My husband had switched to afternoons because he was a very unhappy person working nights. It was really nice having my dad watch the baby for the one hour while my husband left for work, and I was driving home. Remember, at the beginning of the story, I didn't have a job and I found out I was pregnant. Well, I found a job and waited until my three-month probation was over to tell them about my pregnancy so they couldn't fire me. Well, that came back and bit me in the bum because they replaced me with a self-employed woman, and four weeks after my return to work, they let me go. I know you're probably thinking *they can't do that*, but yes, they could. The owner's sister worked for the labor board, so she made sure to do everything by the book so it wouldn't be against the law. After my termination, I was in the same position again: pregnant, without a job. I found something within three weeks, and I was in the same place. I couldn't say anything, but this time I was seven months pregnant when I told my boss. Lucky for me, his wife was pregnant too, so he was overjoyed for me to be expecting. I worked right up until my due date. I was scheduled for a C-section at thirty-nine weeks. It was easy and I was ready. My parents took care of our oldest son while we were at the hospital having another baby boy. Unfortunately, I got postpartum depression again, and it was really bad this time around. I breastfed him until he was ten months old, but a lot happened in between. We canceled our house contract with my parents early. They bought us out after a year and a half. We took that money and bought our own house further north, out of the city. It was lovely. The day our house closed was the day I went back to work. My boss agreed for me to work seven and a half hours a day because of our family schedule. When things seemed to be going great, something would come up. That is definitely how I lived my life. Six months after we moved into what I thought was our dream home that we were going to grow old in, my husband told me that he hated the house. He only said yes because I loved it and he didn't want to look at houses anymore. We were outbid on eight houses before we got this one. He hated the house, and he hated his job that he had been steadily working at for over three years. We had a great setup. My husband was with the boys in the morning and would drive them to my work, then grab the car I drove to work in, and he would drive around the corner to his job. It worked out perfectly. Then I would drive home with the boys, and we would have dinner, take a bath, and then it was bedtime. I would work out and then get ready for the next day. I really enjoyed that setup. When my husband expressed his dislike, we brought my husband's grandparents to our home from Cuba to look after the boys so I could set up day care and my husband could find a new job. It was nice having them here with us and having so much help. We accomplished everything and his grandparents went home two months later.

We then set out to have a daughter. We had two boys, life was going really well, and I wanted a girl. So, I got a girl. I also lost my job right after I found out that I was pregnant with her. See my pattern? I believed life was hard and life showed me it was absolutely tough. I worked at two places while I was pregnant with my little girl, and I got sick a lot. The boys were easy, but she was not. That's how I knew it was a girl; the pregnancy was much different.

Moving ahead, I had my daughter and took the boys out of day care. The oldest was starting school. My husband was working a new job that he enjoyed, and I was again unemployed. Life was exceptional when I was a stay-at-home wife. I was getting paid by the government and I was at home taking care of business. It was smooth until it wasn't. Again, my husband went through some more blips with his jobs. He worked two jobs for six months so I could continue to stay at home after my maternity payments ended. I couldn't bear watching him suffer, so I got a part-time job that was very accommodating and paid really well. My husband was at home with two kids in the mornings because he was on afternoons again. I would bring the oldest to school, then go to work, and I would work until I had to pick him up from school. As soon as I got home, my husband would go to work. It seemed like it was all working. My husband switched jobs again. I put the two younger kids in day care two times per week and thankfully, my bosses were okay with that. Then the pandemic happened. Luckily, I was moved to working remotely from home. My oldest son was moved to online homeschooling. My husband's job was essential, and the two kids were taken out of day care because I was home. The day cares were closed for months. Life got really hard for me. I'm sure it did for so many people.

CHAPTER 2

My First Self-Improvement Program

My husband and I were not doing very well. This time, he wasn't trying to escape me, but neither one of us was happy in our situation. I hated my life. I was earning less money because I couldn't work as much being home with the three kids all the time. I was no longer enjoying my children because I was around them 24/7. I wanted more from life. I wanted and needed help but couldn't find anyone to take care of my kids while I was at home, working.

There is a saying that when the student is ready, the teacher will appear. That's exactly what happened. I found a webinar about the "Science of Getting Rich," and my husband and I watched it. We were sold by the time the video was over. We made what seemed to be a very expensive purchase at the time, but now, looking back, it wasn't. We both dove in to re-spark our lives. I downloaded all the audio stuff to an MP3 so he could listen to it at work, and I studied every chance I got. I listened to the audio while I worked. I did the questions after the kids were in bed. I went full tilt to get help and get happy. I changed a bit, but my husband didn't change at all.

We still had our weird fights when I was PMSing every month. I found that the whole house ran off the energy I was producing for that day. I knew it was important for me to fix myself. Then maybe I could fix my kids and my husband in the process. I worked hard, read a lot, and bought every book suggested in that program. I still haven't read all of them. But they are there for when I have time. In July 2020, I took a completely different weekend seminar with a different mentor. Unfortunately, this time I attended without my husband because he was watching the kids. That weekend webinar helped me find my purpose. I then said to my husband, "I am going to write a book and help millions of people all around the world." He got so excited for me. I purchased another program showing me how to write, publish, and market a best seller. Once again, I got right into it and started to study the program. I had so many ideas that I had absolutely no focus at ALL. It was pretty frustrating for me and my husband. I was spending, spending, spending, and I was running around in circles, all while raising three kids and making sure my house was clean and there was a hot meal on the table for my husband when he got home from his long, hard day at work. I was pretty successful with all my responsibilities. Well, for the most part. In June 2020, my husband and I wrote a list together about the dream house we wanted. I had done my yearly review from my job and asked them for permission to work remotely on a permanent basis and they said yes. I only had to go into the office to complete a few things on an irregular basis, so I was set. My husband wanted to move out of the town we were living in, and finally, after three years of him poking me to move, I said, "Let's do it." We took our list of must-haves and found an excellent realtor. Then, we started looking at houses. The market was hot so we needed someone who was experienced and would lead us in the right direction. And we found a perfect guy. We spent a couple of weekends with him looking at houses, and he was telling us about the area, the schools, the arena, kids' sports, and day cares. He was well-informed on all the subjects we needed information about. My husband and I both felt like this was the right move. It was where we needed to be. The only thing holding us back was me thinking that my ex-boyfriend lived in this town. I had allowed that guy to control my life for far too long, so I let go and released the fear. We looked at two houses that were at the top end of our budget or just outside of our budget, and we both fell in love as soon as we stepped inside the houses. They were absolutely perfect. They checked off all the boxes from our house lists of wants and needs. The realtor told us the builder was a great builder and we went on with our day. On the way home, we drove right past the builder by complete fluke. You can imagine me slamming on the brakes and pulling into the parking spot. We left the kids in the car and the two of us went into the show home and met this wonderful lady who was the saleswoman on the job. She knew everything—who was moving where, how many people had kids, what ages the kids were. It was incredible! We scanned the walls to find the house we had just gone into, and we priced it all out and then we picked the lot we wanted. It was perfect, except my husband would not sign the papers until our house was sold. I called our realtor as soon as we got home from the sales office and there was a "for sale" sign up on our lawn three business days later. It was fabulous. However, if we would have known about the law of supply, we would have purchased the already built house and moved in within sixty days, knowing that our financing would go through no matter what amount was needed. But we weren't aware of the universal laws so we sold our house and went to the builder and placed a very small deposit on the house. When you're dealing with a new builder, there are specific requirements to fulfill. We could not do so right at the time, so I told the wonderful woman that sold us the house that I wasn't leaving without a house. And we didn't! It was so exciting. The owner approved us to put a small amount down to seal the deal, and the day of our closing on our house we would pay them the full balance instead of installments.

She had called us twice before our house closed to make sure we still wanted the house, and we definitely did. It gave us both something to look forward to.

We were supposed to move in with my parents for the nine months that the house was getting built, but my dad said he wasn't comfortable with that because of the pandemic and all. We needed to find a place that would take us for less than a year. The task was not easy. I looked and was rejected. We wanted to stay close to my husband's work and the kids' school, so we didn't have to move them twice as it didn't seem fair for them. Finally, six days before our closing date, I found a rental unit that would take us for the nine months required. I could have lied and said yes, we will be there for a year and just moved out early, but that's not my style. I believe that honesty is my best policy even if it causes me headaches in the process. We got a beautiful new townhouse. The rent was higher than our complete house we just sold. It was a stretch, but it wasn't my parents', which ended up working out for all of us because our house wasn't built on time. We moved into our rental and closed on the day we said it would. It was a very smooth process. We drove to the builder the next day with the full amount, and it was marvelous.

We were living in our new, much smaller rental. I had two kids being homeschooled online because of the pandemic. They were physically in school for less than two months. The townhouse had an unfinished basement and a small backyard. My kids changed after we moved. They were bad. They stopped having fun and started hurting each other. It wasn't pretty. My oldest son was now in grade one and needed help with ALL of his work and my middle guy didn't get on the Google classroom at all. It was stressful. But I did it. And I'm so proud of me and my kids for getting through all that weird worldwide crazy stuff.

CHAPTER 3

THE PROGRAM THAT CHANGED MY LIFE

In January 2021, I signed up for a free five-day online training, and it changed my life. I bought a $10,000 program, and within three days, I knew this program was meant for me. Again, when the student is ready, the teacher will appear. At the time, I was overweight and not happy with my outside as well as my inside. I didn't like who I had become. I remember telling my husband that I didn't like myself. No wonder I didn't have any friends and my kids weren't getting invited to birthday parties anymore. I felt horrible because I was rubbing off on my kids and they were starting to feel left out. The one good thing about my little family of five is that we do everything together as a family, so my children are used to it being us five. So, when one of their birthdays would come up, we would ask them what they wanted to do. Lucky for me, they always wanted to do something with just the five of us, like spending the weekend in Niagara Falls, renting a cottage up north and having a campfire, going to Cuba, and visiting the family. My husband and I were always more than happy to spend quality time as a family and not have to impress other people and their children. Even our close friends stopped inviting us to their kids' birthday parties, and unfortunately for me, social media told me all about the parties we weren't invited to.

I knew I needed to change. I wanted to change my family tree from just getting by to being extremely happy, healthy, and wealthy. I was moving into a deeper depression after the first program. Yes, it helped my husband and me in figuring out what we wanted in a new house, but it didn't help us with anything else. When I found her, I knew she was sent to me by the universe. She was not your average saleswoman. She was BIG, BOLD, and beautiful. She was confident, well-spoken, and had a team of fabulous women of all different shapes and sizes from all different walks of life. She earned her first million dollars in seven months and her second million in seven weeks. I knew I wanted to learn from her. I reached out to her immediately just to chat about what I was feeling, and after three social media messages, I was sold. I spoke to my husband about it, and he saw the enthusiasm in me about this program. It was a twelve-lesson program that lasted twenty-six weeks, and I would be a part of a group for one whole year. This program would challenge my belief system and reprogram my bad habits by turning them into good habits. It held the promise of helping me to think differently and change my attitude. It would help me earn money and change me and my little family's life. I was in and so was my husband. As I was paying for it, I felt so nervous. I had never spent that amount of money on myself since being married and having a family, and I was using a bit of our down payment for our new house and felt like I was taking away from our kids. How silly was that! It was only $13,500. I did not have a good feeling while I paid for that program, but I did it anyway. And afterward, it felt so good. I got right into the material. I was becoming a professional student. My husband even said he would do the program with me so the money would be well worth it. Deep down inside, I felt like this was going to save my marriage.

This was the last chance; I had no other solution but for my husband and I to change our mindsets together.

We started the program together that following Monday, and it was fantastic. I printed all the material off for him and made us both workbooks. I went and bought binders so everything would be put together and organized. I was waking up every morning at 5 a.m. with my husband, which was his normal time to go to work, but this was very new for me. He usually complained through the video we needed to watch every day and fell asleep to it every night. Then, I would do the workbook and my husband would go to work, or he would go through the questions very fast, like he was just fluffing through them. I knew this program was about deep thinking to change the subconscious mind. Things were shifting for me, but my husband didn't seem interested at all. He wasn't putting in the work. He wouldn't make time to study when he got home from work, and he wasn't watching the replays either. To my surprise, my husband quit the program after four weeks of studying with me. He said I was too intense and he didn't want to study with me anymore. It was heartbreaking. It slowed my progress right down to just about a screeching halt. But I got back up and kept trying. I would wake up on my own after he left the bed, and I would watch the video in our room. I refused to give up. If he didn't want to change his crappy life, that was his problem. I was going for it, whatever the cost.

I kept studying and doing the questions. I kept reading the books. I never missed a training lesson. I attended all the live launch free trainings. I kept making my goals. I was writing my book (a different one), which was something I wanted to do so badly. I created an awesome planner that would help with goal setting, planning your day, week, and month, as well as a gratitude journal. I created it in 2020 and used it to achieve all my goals for eight months. And it totally worked! So, I put the planner online. I thought, "Wow! If this planner created so much success for me, how could I help others achieve their goals that they didn't know they wanted?" I created a beautiful website on paper, bought my domain name, and opened a new email account and a business bank account. I was starting a business and I was determined to be successful. Things were moving along. I was doing coaching calls once a week with my coach. I was attending all the training classes and watching all the old replays to get as much knowledge as possible. I was on fire—making quantum leaps, as they say. I was spending the down payment on my new house like I was a millionaire. The only problem was that I didn't have the belief in myself. I pivoted and got off track after I purchased my new SUV, the dream car I had wanted since I was nineteen years old. When I couldn't afford a private mentorship with the coach I was working with, I went elsewhere for solutions. I thought this person had privately mentored my coach, and I thought this was perfect, because I would get this mentorship from the master anyway. Less than a month after joining the private mentorship with the master, I found out that, in fact, it was not the truth. The truth was that they were close friends, and the person I hired was an accountability partner for my coach. I was devastated by the lie I had sold myself on, and I'd just cost my family another $34,000 from our new house deposit. I stopped everything at this point. I stopped studying, I stopped doing the workbook, and I stopped writing my book. I stopped caring and went backwards. I cried a lot. I felt like a complete failure. My husband was furious with me. I spent all that money and now I was doing nothing to earn it back. I wasn't making any money. I wasn't changing my life. That was it! I gave up on myself. My kids had no idea what was wrong with me. I slept in a lot. I stayed in bed on the weekends until the late afternoon because my husband was with the kids, and I could just hide and be depressed and keep it to myself. I looked and felt horrible on the inside and the outside.

My final private mentorship call was put to me ever so gently. "Dana, you are being destructive and creating bad things for yourself. You need to get yourself out of this." Although I thought it wasn't very helpful at the time, I agreed and moved on with my life. Little did I know that this mentor had paved the path for my understanding of the material, broadened my awareness, and helped me figure out my beliefs and habits. She also helped me re-write the story of my past and release the bad, and I became grateful for the good memories of my childhood.

I started studying a book my mentor had mentioned to me. I immediately fell in love with it and started to build my belief back in myself. I started to build my confidence and I started to dream again. Then I noticed that I was attracting prosperous things again. Knowing I had changed my vibration to what I was attracting made me very happy. My husband told me to just focus on the self-development of the programs and never mind the money, as we would figure things out later. I started waking up early again. I joined a different study group and got a new accountability partner. Things started working for me again. I found my faith. The one thing I had found in February and lost in April was my faith. I started working on being happy every day. I would take the kids to the beach and miss an afternoon of work. I would watch YouTube instead of writing my book. I went for an incredible photoshoot that boosted my vibration and my confidence. I stopped hanging out with people that made me negative and started hanging around more positive people. Then I realized something big. The reason we were not getting invitations to our old friends' homes or birthday parties was because we were not on the same vibration anymore. My husband and I were studying so much. We studied *Think and Grow Rich* by Napoleon Hill. I studied *The Science of Getting Rich* by Wallace D. Wattles. I read Thomas Troward, Neville Goddard, Robert Russell, Peggy McColl, Bob Proctor, Joseph Murphy, Louise L. Hay, Abraham Hicks, Venice J. Bloodworth, Maxwell Maltz, and so many more. My husband read *Think and Grow Rich* every day, while I was studying the programs that I had purchased, and every time he read it, he would get something different out of the book and we would discuss it. I kept reading so many more books. I became obsessed with reading. All the knowledge and lessons from all the greats that came before me had made a clear path. I had fallen in love again. I started to change my beliefs and get different results. I was thinking better thoughts, smiling more, and having more fun with my family.

CHAPTER 4

LEARNING THE NATURAL LAWS OF THE UNIVERSE

As my husband and I were studying all the great books from the early 1900s, the ones that taught the same things but in different ways with different words, we came across the natural laws of the universe. At first, we didn't realize what we had found, and it was a bit confusing. Who knew the universe had natural laws? It made so much sense; that was how successful people became successful. That is why so many people just float through life without a real purpose. When we found the laws, we realized this was life-changing in so many ways. We just needed to figure out how to use it to our advantage, just like all those successful people that came before us. We had so many 'aha' moments while learning about these laws. I bought every book I could. I read any article online that would give me examples or a greater understanding of how to use these universal laws to my benefit, because what I learned studying all the great books of the 1800s and early 1900s was that all these great, very successful, happy, and super wealthy people knew the laws and how to use them for their benefit. Here they are! You might want to take notes so you can research them on your own and become exceptionally successful and extremely wealthy as well. Everyone deserves to be happy. I believe that, and now you need to believe that.

#1 The Law of Oneness

Everything just is. We are all a part of divine oneness. I AM is GOD. Do lots of research on this one and it will change your life when your awareness expands to know you are a part of something so big and you are always co-creating and are never alone. You will also discover that everything is already here; we just need to become aware of it.

#2 The Law of Attraction (also known as the Law of Vibration)

This law is so powerful that you could earn a million dollars in a weekend if you really wanted to. You could build the belief and you could actually earn it if there were no counteracting thoughts. This means a lot of study on your part. That way, you can know for sure that it is possible, because so many people have done this. I met a wonderful and super successful person who has earned a million dollars in forty-five minutes.

I have spent a lot of time learning this law and learning how to use it for my benefit. Everything is moving. Nothing ever rests. That is vibration. Take a look at everything around you. You are vibrating with the same frequency as what you see around you. Your table and chairs vibrate. If you can change your frequency, you can change your whole life. This means that changing your thoughts, your feelings, and your frequency will change your results and your life. The easiest way to put it is that your frequency is like a radio station you are living your life on. Please look this one up. It is so interesting to read and know about all the explanations for the law of attraction/vibration. Change your vibration and change your point of attraction.

#3 The Law of Cause and Effect

I love teaching my kids this one because everything we do has an effect. If you're in business and you don't reach out to people daily, how are you supposed to grow your business? It's not going to happen.

If you are mean to your friends, the effect is that they won't want to speak to you anymore.

If you are confident and radiant and you have a great attitude, people will be drawn to you anywhere you go. If you give generously, you will always have enough. This implies that what you give out, always comes back to you. So, always choose what you are giving and what kind of vibration you are emitting wisely.

#4 The Law of Rhythm

I had a problem with this law for a long time. I would have a great time and be productive and have an excellent attitude towards life for two weeks out of the month and then I would have two crappy weeks. My husband and I would fight. I wouldn't want to get out of bed. I was always tired and cranky. It turns out that it's a universal law that I did not understand. When I figured out my body's rhythm, I would check off more of my things to do when I was feeling good, and when I was low, I would sleep more and expect less from myself. My life would work a lot better, and so would my relationships.

The law works just the same in business, but most people use this against themselves because they are observing too many things with the five senses. If your business is having a low sales point, never worry about it, because it's the calm before the storm. Rest and prepare for all those sales that are coming because it is the law. Some weeks are slow. Use those weeks to create and set up, or stock up. Whatever your business, be prepared for that wave of sales that is coming. It is a law. Don't ever get discouraged when your sales are down. Get excited, because the universe is bringing more clients or customers your way, whatever field you are in. Get thrilled about it!

#5 The Law of Relativity

This law, thankfully, you can always use in your favor. Nothing is big or small—only your perception makes it so. For example, $1,000,000 compared to $1,000 is a big amount, but when compared with $10,000,000, it's a smaller amount. Using this law in your favor means using it to boost your belief and faith. There is always someone that is better than you at something. But you are always better at something than someone else is. Use this law to build yourself up. Build powerful beliefs, because you truly are limitless. You just need to believe in yourself.

#6 The Law of Polarity

This law means that there are always two sides to everything. Think of a pole or a stick. You are either happy or you're not. You can't be both. You are either up or down, front or back. So, when you think of something bad and it makes you sad, think of something that would make you happy and move to the other side of the stick. It's really that simple. You can't be angry in a state of gratitude. You can't be anxious when you are knowledgeable. You can't be afraid when you are in a state of faith and belief.

#7 The Law of Gestation (also known as The Law of Gender)

The Law of Gestation or Gender is an interesting law. The way I understand it, the conscious mind is masculine. It has the ability to accept or reject any idea. The subconscious mind is the feminine. It only has the ability to accept the idea. Both masculine and feminine are needed for life to exist. The idea comes from the masculine, but the feminine is the creator. That is why when you get the idea, you MUST put feeling into the idea and the vision. The subconscious mind doesn't know what is real or what is imagined. That is how some people manifest what they want so quickly. They use this law to plant the seed and nurture only the growth. You would not pull up a carrot seed to see if it's growing after a week. It takes about seventy to eighty days for it to germinate and grow into a good-sized carrot that we can pull from the ground and eat.

Another example would be pregnancy. When you get pregnant, it takes 280 days for the baby to be born. That is the gestation period.

Take this law for your goals to manifest. When you create a new goal, always attach a date to it. That way, you do the action part to move towards your goal as the universe moves and forms the matter and substance to bring the goal to you at the same time. It's a magnetic force. No one knows exactly when their goal will manifest, they just know that it will manifest. It is the law. The more belief you have in the goal manifesting, the faster the goal will show up in the physical. That is why we study every day, to build our belief systems that we need to manifest everything we want or can possibly imagine. The universe really wants to give us everything we want. That's why we should only think positive thoughts.

One strong fact that I learned this year as well is "NO MATTER WHERE YOUR RESISTANCE LIVES, THE UNIVERSE WILL ALWAYS FIND A WAY AROUND YOUR RESISTANCE TO GIVE YOU WHAT YOU WANT." So, stay focused on your goal or desire. Happy, sad, angry, or joyful, you will attract whatever you want to you.

CHAPTER 5

GRATITUDE, STUDYING, AND WRITING THOSE LINES

Gratitude

Gratitude is something most of us probably don't even think of, unless something out of this world happens. Would you ever say thank you to the universe for your morning coffee, or the hot shower you just took? That is exactly what feeling gratitude is. In my program, I learnt how to feel deep gratitude and appreciation for everything I have manifested into my life. Because YES, everything you see around you right now was once a thought in your mind that has become a manifestation. As the saying goes, why would someone give you more if you are not grateful for what you have now? If you want to bring more into your life, you must be grateful for what you have. Even if it's not what you want now, it's what you wanted in the past. I heard this somewhere and it really made me think of my life and how I have been living day to day, watching all the things going on around me. It helped me move into my future a lot faster when I understood this concept. What you are looking at now, is yesterday's thinking. Your kids fighting, a huge lineup at the store when you are already late for your meeting. It's all yesterday's thinking. That is why it is so important for you to think good thoughts ALL THE TIME. I watched a You-Tube video about the contamination process. When you take a glass of water and put a dark pop substance into the glass, the water goes dark really fast. Think of that as being your positive mind with a negative thought. But, if you take a dark pop substance and run water into it, it takes a lot of time for the pop to turn into a clear liquid. That's exactly like positive thoughts. Most of us are born and raised with negative thinking patterns and our thoughts are on autopilot. We must purposefully train our minds to think and be positive and happy all the time. It truly is a choice. Those people walking around with a smile 24/7 have trained their minds to be happy and positive, or they were raised in a very positive, happy environment. Unfortunately, most of us grew up like me, watching, hearing, complaining, and becoming the negative thinker that we are today. It's easy to throw out a couple of complaints when you have been hearing it all day. My kids complained all the time. That was a direct reflection of my old thinking pattern. What I was thinking yesterday or the day before, whenever it was, it was my past thinking. When you wake up in the morning, make a conscious decision to speak, act, and feel from gratitude and you will never have a bad day again, because you can't feel gratitude and be negative. You can't be thinking about that guy that just cut you off if you are thinking about that woman who just bought you your coffee in the drive thru. It's wonderfully magical. If you are in a bad mood or someone has just said something to make you tick, you must walk away and start being grateful. "I am grateful for my health, my job, my lunch, and that yummy coffee I had this morning for breakfast" (or on your way to work). A grateful person is a master manifester. Nothing works better than being grateful for something you don't even have yet. Can you imagine? "I am so happy and grateful for my 2018 black Mercedes-Benz GLE 400." I wrote that down. I said it. I pretended that I was driving it when I was cruising down the road in my Grand

Caravan. You know what happened. The universe gave me gut feelings, as I call them, but it's really called intuition, which is one of our higher human faculties. Then, I found the exact SUV I wanted, with the fuel economy that I wanted, and at the exact price I was expecting to pay. That is magic! I laughed at the sales manager when she took my credit card. I told her that I had written this amount down on my goal list of the money I wanted to earn for the life I was creating. And this was the exact amount. The universe wants you to have everything you want. But you must discipline your thoughts to get what you want and stop manifesting all the things you don't want.

After we bought our house, we were waiting for it to be built. Every morning, I wrote down five things I was grateful for and five things I didn't have yet that I was also grateful for. Yes, that means every day I wrote, "I am so grateful for my dream house at such and such address." And I felt so happy and grateful for it already, even though I wasn't living in it. I still pretended I was already living in it, even though I was still living in the townhouse rental, and I was grateful for it. Picture yourself living in your dream house even if you are not. Doesn't that feel great? How can you feel bad if you're living in your imagination all day long with everything that you have ever wanted or dreamed of having? I was always proud of myself before I even finished writing this book, because I knew I would do it and it would be a great success.

Gratitude is a great attitude. If you're ever fighting with your spouse, do yourself a favor. Sit down and write down ten things you love about your spouse and that you are grateful for.

For example, if you are so mad that you can't think of anything, please write down, I am grateful for my spouse because he or she gave me children, or made this nice home. We picked this dining room table out together, and I really like this dining room table. Or maybe you could feel grateful for the life they built with you. That is what I do. I look around me and think to myself, "He is my best friend. I love him and I respect him. We have three healthy, amazing children together. We purchased this dream house together. It was not only my dream house, but we both made sure it was his dream house as well. We went out and bought this great couch together and this couch is so comfortable. He supported me when it was just a thought. He believed in me until my thought became a reality." Then I'm not upset anymore. When I feel gratitude towards my husband, it makes me fall in love with him all over again. Whatever makes you feel better, write it down, say it, think it, and be grateful for your spouse. It will end the argument because you cannot be in gratitude and upset at the same time. It is the law. If you're wondering about your spouse, they feel your energy change towards them. It's just like feeling someone behind you, staring at you. This is also a part of that vibration thing I mentioned in the previous chapter about the laws. If we studied the laws in high school, I don't think anyone would get a divorce or get fired from a job, because we would all know exactly what we wanted and how to go for it without settling for anything less than we desired.

If you are really down and out, and I know I have been, then go back further into your childhood for that gratitude feeling. Maybe you got a doll or toy truck for your birthday. Be grateful for that. Be grateful for the education you have, the safe house you grew up in. If you didn't grow up in a safe house, then be grateful for being alive and well. Know that you can change the trajectory of your tomorrows. You can change your future if you change your thoughts today. Be grateful for that boy in grade ten who explained in a bit more detail how to solve the math problem on the chalkboard. Or that girl who helped you in science because you would not cut the poor frog open. Those are acts of kindness, and if we think about those things, then more of those types of things will happen to us. Just try it; it will prove itself.

Study

Let's talk about study. Oh, I love to study. I study something every day with no excuses and no exceptions. And to be honest, I am kind of obsessed now. I love learning something new. I love building my belief in myself and in the universe. The bigger your manifestations get, the more study you will need. Since study is what helps you move towards a goal and close the gap between you and your goal, it is the law of attraction working in your favor again. As you move yourself towards your goals, the law of attraction is moving your goals towards you. If you knew how to achieve your goal, it wouldn't be a goal at all. A true-blue goal is one that scares you and excites you all at the same time, and you have no idea how you are going to achieve it. But that's the whole point here. The more you study, the more you build your faith and your belief. The "how" will be revealed by the universe. That is what the Law of One is. Universal intelligence. The answers come to us in the form of intuition. What a wonderful concept! Don't you think? Make huge goals and watch the universe move you towards your goals. It's magical. After you become your own master of manifestations, people around you will start to think you're magic. Hopefully, they will ask you how you're getting it done. The more you study, the easier it is to talk to others about thoughts becoming things without them looking at you like you're a weirdo. They will get interested and listen to what you have to say. The more you live this stuff, the faster you will bring your thoughts to yourself. Your goals will get bigger, and you will be able to live the happy, healthy, and wealthy life you always thought was out of your reach.

Writing those lines down

Now, what does "write those lines down" mean? Well, I worked on becoming a *New York Times* best-selling author for over a year. Do you want to know why? Because I didn't write my lines, otherwise known as writing your affirmations.

I would put no time or effort into writing my affirmations. I didn't have time. I didn't think I needed to. I thought it wasn't going to do anything for me because I was acting in a mechanical form. I was fooling myself. As soon as I hit the floor for the millionth time, I said to myself and my husband at that particular point that I was willing to do whatever I had to do to become successful and achieve my goal. I saw others around me writing books and releasing them. They were becoming best-selling authors and I was still in the process of writing. I became committed and I started writing my lines/affirmations every day. I wrote, "I am so happy and grateful now that I am a *New York Times* best-selling author" fifty times a day. I would write until my hand fell asleep. Then I would shake it all about and I did the Hokey Pokey until my lines were all done every day for a week. Do you want to know what happened???? I planted the seed in my subconscious mind that I was a *New York Times* best-selling author and I naturally just started getting great ideas for books. I got the cover design made to what my intuition had offered me. I got inspired action from universal intelligence and I started writing my heart and soul on the paper. It was all inspired action. I did not force myself at all. I stopped forcing myself to write because nothing good came of it. When I started writing my lines or affirmations (whatever you decide to call it) down on paper with a pen every day and feeling like I was a *New York Times* best-selling author, I started getting inspired with so many awesome ideas. That's how this book was written. At 1:31 a.m. on a Sunday night, right after I finished writing my lines, I got the inspiration to write. I started writing and I loved everything that was being expressed out of me. I hope you enjoy reading this as much as I enjoyed writing it for you. In my household, we will continue to say that it is extremely important to be writing your lines, because this momma needed that step to become successful with her goal. I needed the lines to inspire the action which gave me this book. And I can't believe I refused it for so long. You can do this for anything, might I add. If you want money, then you can write, "I am so happy and grateful now that I have XXXXXXX dollars of personal income doing what I love." Yes, please be specific. I watched somewhere that a woman asked to be surrounded by money and she wasn't specific. Well, she ended up getting a job at a bank counting the money. Oh boy! She was surrounded by money, but it wasn't hers. So, be specific. The universe loves clarity. Heaven's first law is an organized mind. I was always told by my coaches that Order is Heaven's first law. Well, finding order took me months, and the coach never explained it to me before our sessions were over, so I asked the big coach while she was teaching us one Tuesday morning. The way I understand Order as Heaven's first law is, get your thoughts straight. Find focus. Pick one thing and work on it. Once that thing is done, move on to the next thing. That's when we co-create the best—with disciplined thoughts and focus. If you want health, you can write, "I am so happy and grateful now that I have complete and perfect health and I look and feel great every day." If you want a house, that's easy too. All you have to do is think of everything you want in a house and start your affirmation with, "I am so happy and grateful now that I am living in my dream home." Whatever you want, make sure you write it down. If you have an address, even better. As Neville Goddard said, start living in the house in your imagination. If you want, at the end of your affirmation, write "Thank you God, it is so," or "Thank you, thank you, thank you." This step is to solidify your goal and acknowledge our creator. Universal intelligence will get the point. The whole secret to all of this is feeling like you already have whatever you're asking for. While you are writing, feel like you have it in your possession already, like you are the person you want to be in your future, today. Act as if you are or have that which you seek already, like you own the business you want to own, or have the money in the bank that you want to spend. Imagine spending that money that you have asked for. Never mind focusing on your debt and bills, or on your current bank balance.

Remember, that was past thinking. Today, you are creating. You are no longer living on autopilot. Give yourself a high five. Feel proud. You are changing your future and your family tree. You got this! Just a tip: prosperity is the feeling you have after the money is spent. So, be thankful buying whatever you buy, and the money will surely circulate back to you. That is what money is for—circulation. You get money and spend money. You get more money and spend more money. Be grateful for all the money you receive and all the money you spend. More will come into your life or experience however you see it. I built the belief that when I spend money, it comes back to me in an amount three times greater. What a wonderful belief, because with money, you can help others. I could write a whole chapter on money, but I won't. I will, however, encourage you to read the book *You Too, Can Be Prosperous* by Robert Russell. There are many different covers for it, but it is an outstanding book, and it will also clear up any and all the false beliefs you might have about money. Hey, you never know—you might even find some beliefs you had about money and never even knew they were down there hiding in your subconscious mind. It will also help you bring more money into your experience. Please read it repeatedly. Each time you study that book, you will get more and more good stuff from it. I have read it twice and studied it once. It helped me so much with all my money beliefs.

What I mean by studying the book is to sit down with your high-lighter, pen, and paper. Read a paragraph and highlight the important parts that mean something to you. Think about what you just read. Does it mean anything to you? If so, write it down. Take notes about what you got from that paragraph. How did it make you feel? Write it down. You are more likely to remember it that way.

CHAPTER 6

COMMITMENT VERSUS CONVENIENCE

I have attended hundreds of free online trainings offered by anyone that I knew had a great reputation and was successful with producing results for themselves. I never quite understood what this statement meant. And then, I found out the hard way. I was doing whatever was convenient for me. I passed on the daily study, I didn't do the workbook daily, and I had no interest in writing my lines, my affirmations. I was not committed at all, until I became desperate. I had moved along, stagnant for so long that I just couldn't take my results anymore. Every month that passed made me feel more and more like a failure. I made a committed decision to quantum leap my results and get it done. No more excuses, no more stalling, no more procrastinating. I was all in, and this was happening for me, because I deserved great results just like all these other people I was studying with.

I started getting up early every morning—and not just sometimes, but all the time. On weekends, I would sleep in. But you better believe I got my butt out of bed early in the morning from Monday to Friday. I was on those study calls. I did the workbook every day. I answered the same questions over and over again to change my deep-rooted beliefs. I recorded the life I wanted onto my phone and listened to it all day, every day, just to get it into my subconscious mind. I wrote my lines. I started getting inspired action and I started committing to do it. And guess what? My results changed and I did it. Whatever I said I was going to do the night before or the morning of, it did not matter how busy I had been during the day or how tired I was, I was committed to doing it every day and finally getting the results, once and for all. And then once I achieved my first goal, I moved down the list. I happily started working on the next goal and I built my confidence in myself back to where it should have been in the first place.

This works with so many things we do in our day-to-day life. For example, if your goal is to lose ten pounds, you must want to eat healthier and exercise more often. So, your affirmation could be, "I am so happy and grateful now that I am 154 pounds, and I am healthy, vibrant, and filled with energy." That is what you write down on the paper, and your subconscious will take it and start automatically changing your eating habits and your snacking favorites. This is why so many people go on a diet and say that they are going to lose weight, but always end up eventually finding the weight again, because your autopilot subconscious mind says, "Hey, what's going on? Now let's eat this extra Halloween candy and some ice cream to find the weight you lost." Always say, "I am releasing weight." That way, your very brilliant mind doesn't go looking for it again and it will help keep the weight off. I have done this in the past and I have also gained weight like this. I saw myself as fat, so my mind said, "Okay, that's the way you see yourself, so here it is. Your wish is my command." One of the great writers that I love to read, Neville Goddard, calls it our secret self. Can you imagine? We are what we see ourselves to be in our hearts. So, if we want to be confident, we need to tell ourselves that in the mirror every day and record it on our phone and listen to ourselves telling ourselves that we are confident and powerful. That way, it becomes automatic. The secret is that you MUST feel confident and see yourself as confident. Otherwise, you are just affirming to your subconscious mind that you are not confident. Our minds are so incredible. I can't even begin to tell you how great we humans were built by our creator. Do your own research, and you will fall in love with yourself and how incredibly you were created. The mind, the brain, the conscious mind and the subconscious mind, our bodies—we are all so magical. Our creator truly knew we would be so special and different from any other species on this planet.

At the end of it all, you must commit to yourself that you will do whatever needs to be done in order to achieve your goals. That is the only way you will get there. Just so you know, there is a secondary law that is the Law of Non-Resistance. My husband and I live our lives by that, especially when negotiating with our children. If you have beliefs that are blocking you from your goal, universal intelligence will move you around all obstacles to get you to your goal, no matter what. Napoleon Hill, in his book, *Think and Grow Rich,* says, "The obstacles must give way." It is the law. Those perfect laws that we should all learn in school, right? That's exactly what I thought when I was studying the laws. Why don't we learn things like this in school? It is a life skill, but you need to learn it on your own, and if you aren't aware of them even existing, how are you supposed to go searching? You are guaranteed success in all areas of your life. When you put it out to the universe, it will start showing clues and evidence. All you need to do is just look for it. The evidence is out there. Build the beliefs, and maintain trust in your faith. The universe will always provide. Commit to it and watch your beautiful new life unfold right in front of your eyes. It truly is magical, and you 100 percent deserve it. You deserve to be, do, and have anything you want. You are enough and you will always be enough. As I tell myself, "HELL YES, I AM WORTHY!"

CHAPTER 7

MY RESULTS FROM HIRING A MENTOR AND A COACH

My life has changed completely. I have a different relationship with my husband; we are flourishing and totally in love. I have a beautiful relationship with all three of my children, and it is fabulous. They are all so wonderful and I am proud to be their mother. Our house is built. My husband quit his job and loves what he is doing now because he did the program with me. FINALLY! We have been able to help our family in ways we never thought possible before. I know exactly how to get what I want and manipulate energy in positive ways. We have been on wonderful vacations and romantic getaways. I manifested the most perfect babysitter for our children. I love my purses and my SUV and my business. I created all of it, and you can too. Remember, all coaches and mentors believe in their products and services. They all believe that they are the best at what they do. They all want to help you live the life of your dreams and are excellent salespeople, but do what is best for you. Find the coach and/or mentor that you click with, that speaks to you and helps you understand the world you never knew existed. Or maybe you knew it existed but didn't quite understand it. I feel so blessed that the one program I joined exposed me to many, many different coaches, mentors, and programs, which all had a significant role in helping me with one thing or another. Two of the coaches even helped me with my kids. One coach helped me work through my insecurities. One coach educated me on self-love. One mentor and program showed me how to write this book and market it. One coach taught me that I was so special and helped me realize why I went through every single thing I went through growing up, in order to become the amazing person I am today. Three coaches and three mentors helped me find my purpose. I will share that figuring out that one thing changed my life completely. I stopped being afraid of change and started working toward becoming who I was supposed to be. Man, I can tell you it changed everything in my life, my mood, and my surroundings. I am so grateful for all the wonderful people who have helped me along in this journey. One woman I met on a training reached out to me to show me how to spoon my feet to balance my energy throughout the day. She is an incredible woman too. I'm so blessed. I have also met so many multimillionaires that I know exactly how I want to live my life and my husband is on board and excited for our future just as much as I am.

The knowledge you will get from a coach or a mentor, no matter if they were the right fit for you or not, is knowledge you will never lose. You can use that knowledge however you see fit. And the people you meet in a mentorship program make it worth it as well. Surround yourself with strong, successful, ethical, and moral people and you become limitless. I have built wonderful, solid friendships that I never would have come across if I didn't pivot. I never gave up on myself. I kept moving forward no matter what.

This year I have challenged most, if not all, of my beliefs, even the things that were completely buried because I formed them when I was a child. I have analyzed my personality without judgment, my thoughts, and my purpose here on earth. I have built my faith, changed the angry, sinful man I once believed in as a small child until the age of thirty-seven, and built an image of I AM GOD, just like the books I read repeatedly said. And I will continue to read them repeatedly. I am not here to change your faith or your religion, but I have learnt over the past twelve months that God/spirit/universe/universal intelligence/light/our creator, whatever you want to call it (I choose 'God'), wants us all to have everything we have ever wanted. Our creator (God) wants us all to succeed, to fulfill our purpose, and be all that we can be. Spirit (God) loves us unconditionally just the way we are. Think about that for a minute. That's really powerful. Think of all those people unhappily working in a job that they hate because they think they can't do better. Don't be one of those people. Think your way to the top. Be like me and all those other weird people that I joined eighteen months ago. Try it out! I guarantee you will not want to go back to the 95 percent of people who would rather die than think. I dare you. Just start with one thing. A beautiful woman who was taking the program with me used a perfect example to build the belief system: focus on flamingos. Think only of flamingos, and you will start to see them everywhere you go. You might see a real one, depending on where in the world you are. You might see a picture of one. One might pop up on your phone as you are mindlessly scrolling. You might even see a sticker on a car's window that you drive by today or tomorrow. You never know, but the universe will bring a flamingo to you somehow, in some way. My experience with the flamingo exercise happened like this. My husband and I were checking off a goal on our list and we were at a family resort playing in the arcade with our three kids. I looked at a machine that you win toys in, and there it was! A beautiful pink flamingo with blue sparkly eyes and a gold beak. You bet I won that flamingo, and it sits on my dresser now in my bedroom. Every morning when I wake up, I see it, and every night when I go to bed, I see it again. That beautiful little Beanie Baby flamingo represents belief in myself, in the universal intelligence, and in my faith. What an incredible thing to wake up to every morning! I have only ever seen one flamingo that was flying with its wings wide open, beautifully gliding freely in the sky. I still remember the way I felt. It was incredible. I was dating my husband and we were driving back to the resort from his house. I had just met his family for the first time. I would have jumped out of the car with excitement if we weren't driving on a bridge, surrounded by water. My husband (then boyfriend) was completely confused. He had seen them all the time driving to and from work. That was the very first time I had ever seen one in real life. Since then, we have only seen flamingos at the zoo. But since that very first time that I saw that beautiful pink and white bird flying through the sky, soaring just above the aqua-colored Cuban ocean, I was completely taken aback by it. And I still am, to the day I can get a picture of a real, flying flamingo. I toast to your success. All the time, effort, and especially money, was absolutely worth it for the people I have met, the lessons I have learned, the wonderful business I have created, the way I feel about myself, and the knowledge I have now. I would do it all over again in a heartbeat.

I found my faith in God.

I found my purpose.

I saved my life.

I saved my marriage.

My husband found his purpose.

We both got to change our family trees, because my husband came from lack and limitation, as well as a very impoverished country. He had a poor mindset—so poor that when he came to Canada, we sat on camping chairs as our living room couch. He didn't believe we should spend the money on a couch for our comfort because he never had one back home. Yes, you know the ones that you buy at the big box store. They have fabric with metal legs and fold into a convenient bag so you can easily take them on a camping trips. Yep, one and the same. For three whole months, we sat on those, until my cousin gave us her old couch that we had to drive two and a half hours one way to pick up. And I was pregnant, so I couldn't even help him get it into my dad's van. What a man that guy is! I am very excited to tell you that after eight years of my husband living in Canada and going through these programs with me, he has a prosperity and abundance mindset, and we finally bought our very first brand-new sofa and loveseat set just before we moved into our new house. It was so exciting to go shopping for something new. Until now, we only got things given to us and used by others. The feeling of walking into the store and trying the couches out to see what we liked, and then ordering the couches was amazing. Woohoo! We went from going to people's houses and thinking their furniture was so nice, but that we could never afford it, to YES, we can do it. Money is abundant. I want those ones. I also got the pleasure of buying the appliances that I wanted, not because they were the cheapest at the store. I bought the ones I wanted and I'm so excited to have a fridge that I love, in the color that I want, with the shelves that I need for my family. I am also grateful for the matching stove and dishwasher in the color that my husband and I love.

My children are changed forever because my husband and I are so blessed to share our knowledge with them. The great thing about them being so young is that their subconscious minds will take it as truth and believe it until they, too, challenge the belief when they get older. I love teaching them about the laws of the universe, as well as thought energy. It is so much fun seeing the way they understand it. The beliefs we are instilling in our children will help them create happiness, health, and lots of wealth for them when they grow up, and I am so proud to be their mother and watch them grow into whatever success they become.

Thank you so much for reading my book. I hope you get a lot of value from these words. I hope you study the laws and join an awesome program that changes your life, just like it did for me. I wish you so many terrific things. I wish you all the best in your life. I have so much gratitude now and forever. Remember, if you can't be grateful for what you have now, how can you be grateful for what you want and are manifesting into your life? Good luck, and remember:

YOU ARE PROSPERITY! Say to yourself, "I AM PROSPERITY" one hundred times a day.

YOU ARE ENOUGH! Say to yourself, "I AM ENOUGH" one hundred times a day.

YOU ARE WORTHY! Say to yourself, "I AM WORTHY" one hundred times a day.

YOU ARE HAPPY, HEALTHY, AND WEALTHY! Say to yourself, "I AM HAPPY, HEALTHY, AND WEALTHY" one hundred times a day.

You can change your life, but only if you are "willing" and you are "able!"

If you don't have the belief in yourself, I will lend you my belief in you and the material I have learned. That is how my coaches and mentors have raised me up. They believed in me because they believed in the material they were teaching. They have lived it and so have I. You can do it too.

Thoughts really do become things. You just need to flip your thoughts to only positivity, and thankfully, success has left us clues all throughout the generations. You just need to read and find the clues.

Remember, books are your all-weather best friends!

Thank you so much!

NEVER GIVE UP ON YOURSELF. YOU ARE WORTH IT!

ABOUT THE AUTHOR

Dana Diaz Bermudez is a motivated, self-made woman—a talented entrepreneur who has researched the universal laws, thought processes, and the power of the mind extensively. Her curiosity and thirst for growth led her to Bob Proctor. She then studied multiple programs with the Proctor Gallagher Institute, which guided her to Peggy McColl. This chain of events changed her life and steered her on a spiritual journey to find her purpose in life. She now dedicates her life to helping millions around the globe with her books, programs, and coaching.

Dana is currently working on completing her third book, and has also designed a planner based on goal setting, which helped her achieve massive success in one year just by putting her goals on paper and executing them on a monthly basis. She holds a study group for people to read together and embody the material. Dana also holds monthly mastermind groups to help people express their true selves through their creativity, and has realized that each person brings something fresh and valuable to each group.

With every donation, a voice will be given to
the creativity that lies within the hearts of
our children living with diverse challenges.

By making this difference, children that may
not have been given the opportunity to have their
Heart Heard will have the freedom to create
beautiful works of art and musical creations.

Donate by visiting

HeartstobeHeard.com

We thank you.